D1452660

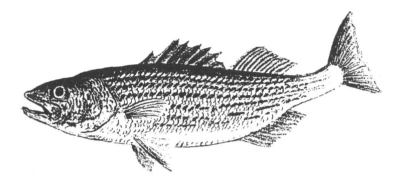

Surf Fishing

by Joe Malat

Joe Malat has more than 25 years of experience catching fish in the surf; several of those years were spent as a professional surf fishing guide on the famed Outer Banks of North Carolina. Joe is an accomplished outdoor writer and photographer, and member of the Outdoor Writers Association of America. His work has appeared in several national and regional publications.

TABLE OF CONTENTS

CATCHING STRIPED BASS

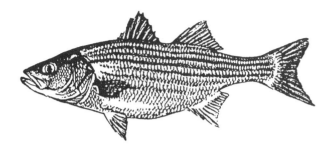

Striped bass are among the most exciting fish to catch from the beach. While some stripers are caught in the surf of the Atlantic coast as far south as North Carolina, most are found north of Delaware. Few fish have the mystique, allure and dedicated following among surf-casters as the striper. They may be unpredictable in their feeding habits. From Delaware south they are called rockfish.

WHERE: Stripers tend to congregate around structure, such as points, jetties and bridges. They are not frequently found along the open beach unless there is something about the bottom profile to hold them in one place. Most surf fishing for stripers occurs along the northeast coast, from Delaware to New England.

WHEN: Spring, summer and fall. They may be caught throughout the day if the fish show a preference for feeding on a certain tide, but most serious striper anglers fish the surf after dark, when larger fish feel more comfortable in shallow water.

HOW: Catch stripers of all sizes on swimming plugs such as Danny Plugs, Gibbs Swimmers or Bottle Plugs, and Atom Striper Swipers. The biggest stripers are consistently caught on live baits such as live eels, hooked through the lips or eyes. Live menhaden can be fished from jetties, but do not cast well from the beach.

TIPS: Fishing hard and often is the best way to catch a striped bass. After dark a slow retrieve is mandatory for live eels and swimming plugs. Stripers can be leader shy. Avoid wire leaders.

SIZE: Stripers are caught in all sizes. The world record on rod and reel is 78½ pounds, and was caught from the surf near Atlantic City, New Jersey. The largest ever recorded weighed 128 pounds, and came from Edenton, North Carolina. Similar sized fish tend to school together.

SWIMMING PLUG

(See page 29)

A PROVEN LURE FOR STRIPED BASS

CATCHING BLUEFISH

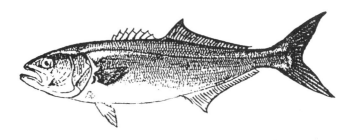

Bluefish are such aggressive feeders that during a blitz (feeding frenzy), baitfish may beach themselves to avoid being eaten by the blues. Blues are migratory. They range from North Carolina to New England, and along the southeast coast of Florida. Their teeth are razor-sharp, so they are to be handled carefully.

WHERE: Near inlets, points, deep holes on the beach, moving water or rip currents.

WHEN: Spring, summer and fall for small blues. South of the Chesapeake Bay, spring and fall are prime times for the jumbos. North of the Chesapeake the big blues are caught in the summer and fall. Incoming water to high tide is best along the open beach. Falling water down to low tide can be productive around inlets, too, as the fish feed on bait being swept out through the inlet. Dawn and dusk are the best times of the day to catch bluefish. Blues will feed after dark.

HOW: When you see "breaking" fish, diving birds or jumping baitfish, cast lures such as hammered metal spoons, top water or swimming plugs. When the surf is rough and the water is dirty, fish with bait; mullet, herring, spot, or menhaden. For the jumbo blues use single hook fireball rigs with 7/0 to 9/0 hooks and two hook fireballs for the smaller blues. In strong currents fireballs do not hold bottom well; use single hooks with wire leaders on a triple swivel rig.

TIPS: Look for "working birds" along the surf line. If the birds are
         working they are after baitfish being chased to the surface by
         the blues. Bluefish prefer to feed in clear water, but if a food
         source is available water clarity is not critical. Use wire leaders
         with dark colored snaps and swivels; bluefish will frequently
         strike at anything bright and shiny.

SIZE: Blues come in all sizes and usually school together according
         to size. Small blues, called "snappers" or "tailors" rarely
         associate with the bigger fish for fear of being eaten. "Jumbo"
         blues can weigh 20 pounds or more. The world record for
         bluefish is 31 pounds, 12 ounces.

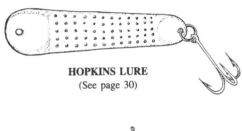

HOPKINS LURE
(See page 30)

BLUEFISH TACKLE

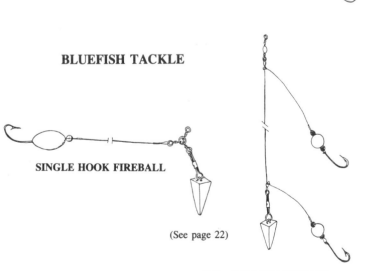

SINGLE HOOK FIREBALL

(See page 22)

DOUBLE HOOK FIREBALL

4

CATCHING FLOUNDER

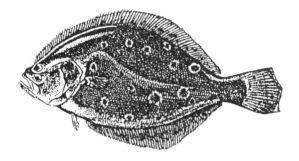

Summer flounder, also known as fluke, are common along most of the Atlantic coast. Winter flounder are infrequently found south of New Jersey. Southern flounder closely resemble summer flounder, and the ranges of both species overlap. The southern and summer flatfish closely resemble each other in their feeding habits, locations and size, so when I mention flounder I am referring to either of these two species. Some folks believe flounder are the best tasting salt water fish, and their firm white fillets receive high marks on the table.

WHERE: Flounder prefer to look for food in narrow sloughs and deep holes, or "pockets", that form on the inside edge of sandbars or along either side of a point. Flounder like moderately clear water, and a calm surf.

WHEN: The larger flatfish are caught in the spring and fall, but they are available practically year round. They can be caught at any time of the day, and stage of the tide is more critical than time. Moving water, generally incoming to high tide, is the best; especially around inlets.

HOW: Bucktail lures of various sizes sweetened with strips of squid or mullet are popular along the entire coast. "Old Salt" fluke rigs, two hook bottom rigs or spinner blade hooks baited with mullet or squid strips are excellent.

TIPS: Flounder stay on the bottom and move very little, even when feeding. Cast your bucktail and bounce it across the bottom, drawing the line back with the rod as you retrieve the lure. Flounder like a moving bait. When fishing with a bottom rig, use a rounded sinker and slowly drag the rig back to you. Light tackle works best, since flounder rarely bite hard; they often just hold onto a bait before swallowing it. Keep bait strips neat. Some anglers use a pair of stainless steel scissors to trim off the ragged edges.

SIZE: Average size for flounder is 1 to 4 pounds, with a rare fish weighing more than 10 pounds.

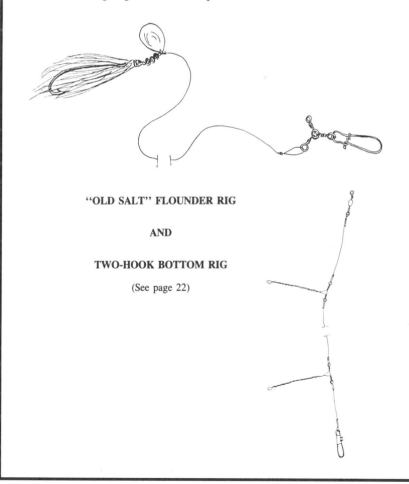

"OLD SALT" FLOUNDER RIG

AND

TWO-HOOK BOTTOM RIG

(See page 22)

6

CATCHING WEAKFISH

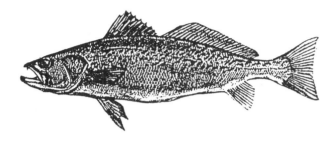

Weakfish are found along the entire Atlantic Coast from New England to Florida, but the greatest numbers of them are caught from New Jersey to North Carolina. The larger fish occur in the northern part of their range. They are also called gray trout, seatrout, weakies, tiderunners and squeteague.

WHERE: Catch weakfish along the open beach, or in narrow, well defined sloughs. They usually travel in large, constantly moving schools, and the key to success is locating the school. They like to feed around structures such as jetties and bridges, where most of the bigger fish are caught. Areas around inlets are good locations to catch weakfish.

WHEN: Spring, summer and fall. They may be caught year-round in the southernmost part of their range. Some good catches may come during the day, but the best action is typically at dawn and dusk, and frequently through the night. Weakfish prefer a moderate to calm surf, and rarely bite well when the ocean is very rough.

HOW: Use lures in clear water. Cast small Hopkins or Stingsilver lures, or lead heads with twister tails. Double bucktail rigs in white, or red and white are productive. Leaders aren't necessary for the smaller fish. When the water is murky or dirty, catch them with squid strips, bloodworms, and strips of cut mullet on bottom rigs. Big weakfish can be caught with live spot, mullet, or menhaden on fishfinder rigs. Live bait fishing for large weakfish is popular from beaches and jetties north of the Chesapeake Bay in the fall.

TIPS: They are called "weakfish" because of their tender mouth tissue. Don't put too much pressure on weakfish as you lead them through the surf, it's easy to pull out the hook. An excellent fish to eat. Their soft meat will spoil quickly, so put them on ice as soon as you catch them.

SIZE: Most surf catches range from 1 to 3 pounds, but larger fish are more common in the northern part of their range. The current world record of 19 pounds, 2 ounces was caught from the surf near Jones Beach, NY.

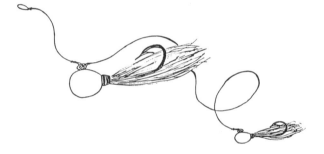

DOUBLE BUCKTAIL RIG

(See page 22)

GOOD LURE FOR WEAKFISH (AND FLOUNDER). MAY BE "SWEETENED" WITH STRIPS OF SQUID.

CATCHING SPECKLED TROUT

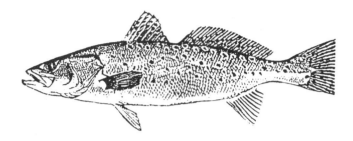

The speckled trout is both a fine game fish and gourmet fare. These attributes, combined with its colorful appearance, makes the speckled trout a very popular fish. Also called specks, spotted sea trout, or trout, because they have a soft, tender mouth many anglers employ light tackle to catch them. They are an inshore fish that spawn in estuaries. Large numbers of them migrate along Atlantic Coast beaches during spring and fall.

WHERE: Catch trout in narrow sloughs, with a bar close to the beach. Look for breaks in the bar and fish the "outsuck", or fast moving water around the break. Look for points with deep pockets on either side of the point, and bar formations that are found on either side of fishing piers.

WHEN: Spring, fall and summer. Early and late in the day. First light of day is preferred by most trout fishermen, and night tides will produce on a full moon. Clear water with a moderate to calm surf is ideal. A good combination is low tide that occurs early and late.

HOW: Fish with lures in clear water. Use MirrOlures in green, or red and white, or lead head jigs with soft plastic. Mr. Wiffle or grub tails can sometimes be rigged in tandem. Popular tail colors are green, white, and pink and white. Double rigged bucktails. In dirty or rough water, fish with cut mullet or fresh shrimp on a two hook bottom rig.

TIPS: When fishing a lure, eliminate any excess snaps or swivels. Trout have few teeth, and will rarely bite through monofilament. If the water is very clear tie lures directly to the line. Trout can change their color preference for a bait almost daily, so don't hesitate to change lure colors frequently, and experiment, if what you are using doesn't catch a trout.

SIZE: The world record speckled trout is 16 pounds. Most weigh far less. Average size is 1 to 3 pounds. A speck that weighs more than 5 pounds is a genuine trophy for surf-casters.

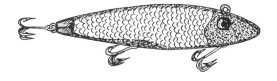

MIRROLURE

(See page 31)

**USE A SLOW RETRIEVE
FOR SPECKLED TROUT**

CATCHING RED DRUM

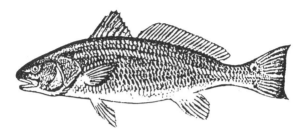

Known on southern beaches as the "king of the surf", red drum are a highly prized sport fish. In different areas they are also known as channel bass, reds, redfish, spot-tails. Smaller fish are called puppy drum. They are bottom feeders, and an excellent target for bait fishermen. Occasional drum may also be captured on lures in the surf. The Barrier Islands of Virginia are their usual northern-most range, however they are caught from every Atlantic and Gulf coast state.

WHERE: Red drum are migratory, but come in close to shore to feed. They prefer to feed in rough, shoal waters found near inlets, passes or swashes, and near prominent points along the beach. On the open beach drum may congregate around breaks in the sand bars.

WHEN: Primarily spring and fall. Red drum like moving water, either rising or falling, and rarely feed on a slack tide. They may come into shallow water to feed, especially after dark. Daybreak and dusk usually see them feeding actively.

HOW: Fish with bait: Fresh mullet, menhaden, and spot, or fresh finger mullet for puppy drum in the early fall. Use fresh shrimp around inlets, especially south of Virginia and in the Gulf; peeler crabs in Virginia. Use fishfinder rigs with monofilament leaders for large drum. Puppy drum will readily bite lead head jigs with soft plastic tails, bucktails, and MirrOlures.

TIPS: Windy days with a choppy or rough surf are more productive for big drum than "bluebird" days, and water clarity is of minor importance. Serious drum anglers will scout out a likely looking beach during the day and return to fish at night. After dark, avoid shining bright lights directly on the water where drum may be feeding. The lights may scare them. Hooks must be sharp; drum have a hard, bony mouth.

SIZE: The world record is 94 pounds, 2 ounces, but most drum are much smaller. Historically, North Carolina and Virginia harbor most of the big drum over 40 pounds.

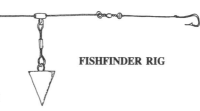

FISHFINDER RIG

BAIT RIGS FOR RED DRUM

(See page 22)

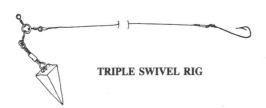

TRIPLE SWIVEL RIG

12

CATCHING KINGFISH

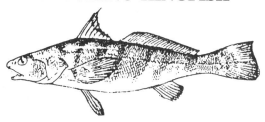

Kingfish are called roundheads in Virginia, sea mullet in North Carolina and whiting in several other states. They are shallow water, inshore fish, and are typically found over sandy bottoms. They are not considered a sport fish, but are important to recreational anglers. They readily take a bait, fight hard, and are prized as table fare. Both species have a single, small chin barbel, but the Northern kingfish has a series of bold, dark bars on its sides.

WHERE: Catch kingfish in narrow sloughs, deep holes or "pockets" that may form on the beach side of the bar, and around cuts or breaks in the outer bar. Sea mullet prefer cloudy water and moderate to rough surf conditions.

WHEN: Spring, summer and fall. Larger fish are caught in the fall and spring, especially in Virginia and North Carolina.

HOW: Fishing with bait is the preferred method almost everywhere. Kingfish are rarely caught on lures, but they may be fooled by a small bucktail tipped with a piece of fresh shrimp, fished on light tackle and tied directly to your line. Bottom fishing with two-hook bottom rigs (hook sizes from #6 to #2), with a monofilament leader, will catch kingfish. Bloodworms are the best bait.

TIPS: They may be caught anywhere from a long cast to a deep hole right at your feet. It pays to fish these two extremes and all of the space in between. Depending on the topography of the beach any stage of the tide may produce, but the fish may fall into a pattern of feeding actively at a certain tide for several days in a row.

SIZE: Kingfish may range to 3 pounds, and fish of varying sizes will readily school together.

CATCHING CROAKER

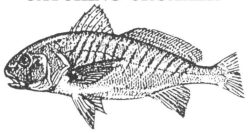

Croakers are not one of the more glamorous species available to the inshore angler, but they are generally dependable, and have salvaged more than one trip when jumbo bluefish, red drum, or speckled trout wouldn't cooperate. They travel in dense schools, and can move in and out of the surf zone with a change of tide or variation of water clarity. Opinions vary as to their desirability on the table. I have found them to be acceptable when fresh, but they develop a strong taste when frozen.

WHERE: Catch them anywhere in the surf, from an open beach with no outer bar to a small, narrow slough.

WHEN: Spring, summer and fall. They may be caught in clear water, but rarely. Large schools of croakers will stay a short distance offshore, and come into the surf zone when the water is dirty. When the water is clear, especially during the summer months, the best catches may be after dark. Stage of the tide is not critical.

HOW: Large croakers are sometimes caught on bucktails or lead heads intended for speckled trout, but most are caught with natural bait fished on the bottom, on two hook bottom rigs with #4 to #1 hooks. Croakers are not picky eaters, and will go for a variety of baits, including bloodworms, squid, shrimp and cut mullet.

TIPS: Croackers will frequently be mixed in with their bottom feeding cousins, the spot. There is no trick to catching them; if they are there, they will bite. They bite hard, and often fight like a much larger fish. When cleaning croakers be careful of a very sharp edge at the back of their gill covers. Their scales are small and difficult to remove.

SIZE: Croakers are small, most weighing ¾ to 1 pound. However, their abundance and size runs in cycles. I have seen croakers caught from the surf that easily topped the two pound mark.

CATCHING SPOT

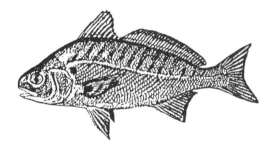

Spot are small members of the drum family. These popular panfish travel in densely packed schools, and tolerate wide ranges of water temperature and salinity. Spot are bottom feeders, and are easily recognized by a small dark "spot" near the top o their head, just behind the gill covers. In Virginia and North Carolina the large, fall-run spot are called "yellow bellies" because of their golden-yellow hue.

WHERE: Almost anywhere in the surf. They bite best in rough, dirty water, especially in late summer or early fall.

WHEN: Summer through early fall. Incoming water to high tide is probably best, but stage of the tide is not critical. With prolonged periods of calm surf and clear water, spot may feed more actively at night.

HOW: Use bloodworms or small pieces of fresh shrimp on two hook bottom rigs, and small #6 to #2 hooks. Cut bloodworms in small pieces that are less than ½ inch long, and thread them on the hook.

TIPS: Spot are easy to catch, and may be caught two at a time, if the school is large. Use small hooks. Spot are one of the most popular panfish in the surf, and are best appreciated on light rods. For their size they fight hard. Catching spot is an excellent way to introduce youngsters to surf fishing.

SIZE: Average size is less than 8 ounces, and a spot that exceeds one pound is a notable catch.

CATCHING POMPANO

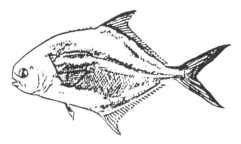

Their true name is Florida pompano, an indication that this fish is a warm water species. They are rare north of the Chesapeake Bay. Their sleek shape, and strong, forked tail enable them to fight hard, and they will often use their deep body to run sideways along the beach when hooked. The light, firm meat of pompano ranks them high on table fare.

WHERE: Catch pompano anywhere along the ocean beach. Pompano feed primarily on small crustaceans in the surf zone, and may forage along the edges of sandbars, or right at the edge of the breaking waves on shore.

WHEN: Pompano are rarely found in water of less then 70 degrees, and can tolerate much warmer water. They prefer clear water, and may feed anytime during daylight hours at any stage of the tide.

HOW: Pompano may be caught on small bucktail jigs tipped with pieces of fresh shrimp, but most are caught on fresh bait. Fresh shrimp and mole crabs, or ''sand fleas'' are favorite baits. Hook sand fleas from their underside up through the top shell. Use two hook bottom rigs, small hooks and monofilament leaders. Snelled gold hooks, rigged with gold spinner blades and beads are popular.

TIPS: Clear water is necessary to catch pompano, but if it's too clear, they may be hard to fool. If that's the case, eliminate as much hardware, such as snaps, swivels, and leaders as possible. Try casting your baited rig out to the sand bar, and move it slowly back, until you find the fish. Pompano will often bite right at your feet, and are fun to catch on light tackle.

SIZE: As large as 8 pounds in Florida, but most of the pompano caught from the Atlantic surf weigh between ½ and three pounds.

CATCHING SPANISH MACKEREL

Spanish mackerel are warm water fish, plentiful from the Chesapeake Bay down to Florida. They move north from Florida as the water temperatures warm in the summer, and may be caught as far north as New York. Most Spanish mackerel are caught by trolling from boats in the near-shore waters, but surf-casters catch them during the summer, especially along North Carolina's Outer Banks. They are strong swimmers.

WHERE: Catch Spanish mackerel anywhere along the open beach. They travel in large schools, and can frequently be located by fish breaking on the surface, and by diving birds. Rarely found in anything but very clear water.

WHEN: Summer and early fall, along most of the mid-Atlantic coast. Prime times are at the first light of day, and again at dusk, with an incoming to high tide.

HOW: Catch them with Stingsilvers in chrome, gold, or pink, or small chrome Hopkins and Kastmasters lures weighing less than 2 ounces. Use a very fast retrieve.
Occasionally skip the lure across the surface when the mackerel are on top. Live finger mullet will catch some of the largest fish in the fall, from beaches near inlets.

TIPS: Spanish are fast swimmers with excellent eyesight. They have teeth, but metal leaders are discouraged. In very clear water it may be necessary to tie the lure directly to your line. Veteran mackerel anglers prefer spinning reels with a fast retrieve, and large spool diameter filled with monofilament line in 10 or 12 pound test. The light line is difficult for the fish to see, and affords good casting distance for the light lures. Their meat is soft, and will spoil quickly if not kept cold.

SIZE: They average from 1 to 4 pounds, but occasionally are larger. The world record mackerel weighed 13 pounds.

INCIDENTAL CATCHES

- There is no way a fisherman can control what type of creature will bite his lure or piece of bait. If an unwanted species is hooked, he shouldn't lose his life for doing what comes naturally . . . eating.

- Carefully unhook and release any unwanted catch. This will benefit the ocean food chain and result in more fish for the future.

SHARKS

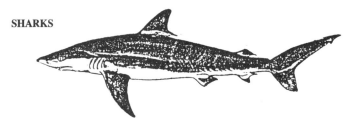

Be wary: Most have sharp teeth. Cut the leader or line as close as possible to the hook, and release the fish.

SKATES AND RAYS

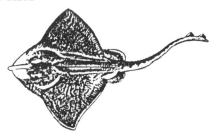

Skates have a shorter, thick tail, with a series of sharp spines from the base to the tip. Skates are not as dangerous as rays, but should be treated with respect and handled carefully.

Rays have a long, thin, whip-like tail with one or more barbs which they use as weapons. These are dangerous, and can inflict a very serious wound. Do not handle rays. Cut the leader as close to the hook as possible and push them back into the ocean with the end of your sandspike.

WHERE TO CATCH FISH IN THE SURF

TIPS:

- Learn to "read the beach" by looking at breaking waves; white water indicates shallow areas, or sand bar formations.

- Scout the beach at low tide when the bars are visible. Note where they are, and return to fish the holes and sloughs (pronounced "slews") at high tide.

- The beach is always changing. Currents, tides and winds shift the sand to form sand bars, holes and flat areas on the beach.

- Look for "breaking" fish (on the surface), jumping baitfish or birds diving on the water.

- When fish feed they often form a slick spot on the water, created by the oils from remains of eaten baitfish.

- Some beaches drop off sharply, and fish may feed along that edge (also called the "drop").

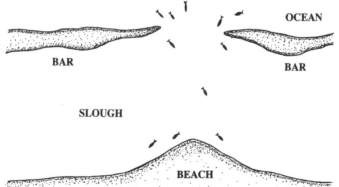

A slough is a trough of deep water between the sandbar and the beach. Fish come into sloughs through breaks in the bar to look for food.

Cast to the break in the bar. The break may be marked by moving, rippling water (rip current), or a slight discoloration of the water on a falling tide, or the absence of cresting waves.

Big blues and red drum prefer wider sloughs. Speckled trout, flounder, and pompano will often be in narrow, deep sloughs.

INLETS AND JETTIES

Also known as passes, inlets are formed where rivers, bays or sounds empty into the ocean.

Fish may feed on baitfish coming out of the inlet on a falling tide, and move into the inlet with an incoming tide.

Rock or wood jetties may be on either side of inlets, or in a series along the open beach.

Jetties attract fish, especially gray trout and striped bass. Cast from the beach, working in a fan pattern from the rocks to the shore along either side of the jetty. Cast from the jetty, if fishing is permitted.

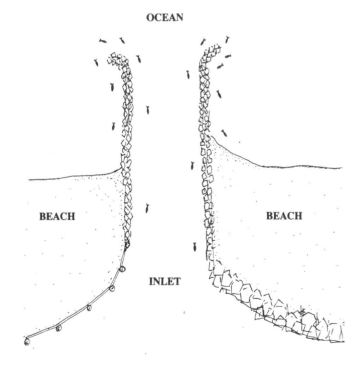

OCEAN

BEACH   BEACH

INLET

POINTS

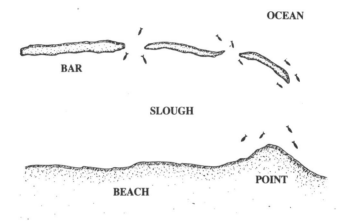

Points may be caused by permanent changes in the shoreline when the land mass changes direction, or may form temporarily with currents, tides, and winds.

Points may form where bar formations come to the beach.

Deep water may be found on either or both sides of a point along the open beach. Fish will be in the deeper water.

RIGS THAT CATCH FISH FROM THE SURF

TWO HOOK BOTTOM RIG

Snap at bottom of the rig permits changing of sinkers as conditions change. Size and type of hooks can be changed to match species of fish. Used for a variety of bottom feeding species, such as spot, croakers, and sea mullet or trout.

TRIPLE SWIVEL RIG

Use wire leader for bluefish. Sinker is attached by a clip to the swivel, and can be easily changed. For red drum and bluefish.

FISHFINDER

Weight attached to the line with a clip that will slide freely. Fish can pick up bait and not feel weight of the sinker. Good for fishing in rough conditions when heavy weights are necessary. Leaders can be wire or monofilament, but mono is used more often. Preferred rig for big red drum.

SINGLE HOOK FIREBALL

Hook size typically 7/0 to 9/0, with wire leader. Float keeps bait moving off the bottom, and is painted a bright color to attract fish. Use cut mullet, spot or other fish for bait. Preferred for big bluefish.

DOUBLE HOOK FIREBALL

Hook sizes from 1 to 2/0. Either wire or monofilament. Popular for small bluefish.

FLOUNDER RIGS

Double bucktails are heavy enough to be cast by themselves, need no additional weight, and catch more fish when "sweetened" with a piece of cut squid or mullet, or a live minnow. The "Old Salt" type flounder rig has a clip for a sinker, and is baited with strips of cut squid, mullet or live minnow. Use a rounded sinker to allow the rig to be moved slowly across the bottom.

HOOKS

Use hooks that suit the fish you are trying to catch. Big fish may bend small, light wire hooks. If your hooks are too big when fishing for small fish, you may get bites, lose baits, and not be able to hook any fish.

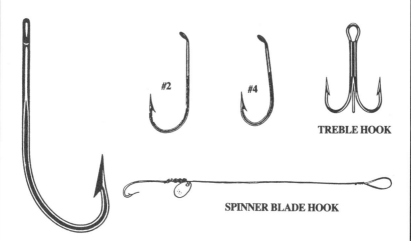

#2

#4

TREBLE HOOK

SPINNER BLADE HOOK

DRUM OR BIG BLUEFISH HOOK 7/0

TERMINAL TACKLE

Snaps and swivels allow for quick, easy changing of lures and rigs, and prevent line twist. They are also used as the heart of several different rigs.

SNAP

SWIVEL

SNAP SWIVEL

A leader is a short piece of monofilament or wire used in front of a lure to prevent fish from biting off the lure. It's connected to the line with a swivel.

TRIPLE SWIVEL

LEADER

SINKERS

TIPS:

- Use only enough weight to keep your rig and bait from moving quickly with the current.

- Too much weight will make hooking fish difficult.

- Some movement is okay as it allows the rig to cover more area.

TYPES OF SINKERS

PYRAMID
Will hold bottom better than rounded weights; the most often used surf sinkers.

ROUND OR BANK STYLE
Allows rig to drift with the currents.

Ideal for flounder fishing. Rig can be moved easily across the bottom.

IN-LINE
May be added in front of a small lure for additional casting weight.

"ENGLISH STYLE"
Wire fingers dig into the sand. When line is pulled tight the wires snap back, and the weight breaks free.

CATCHING FISH WITH BAIT

TIPS:

- Fish feed by sight and smell, so change your bait when it becomes washed out and loses its scent.

- Always keep bait cool and out of the sun.

- When fishing with bait, it's usually not important to hide the hook point.

BAITS THAT CATCH FISH

CUT FISH: MULLET, SPOT, MENHADEN, MACKEREL and HERRING

Use whatever is available seasonally. Fresh bait is always better than frozen, but may not always be available.

Larger baitfish may be scaled, filleted and cut into strips to match the size hook and species. A scaled fillet is easier to put on the hook.

Smaller baitfish may be cut into steaks or chunks.

BLOODWORMS

Careful! Four sharp pincers at the head and will bite.

Bloodworms are salt water marsh worms. They are alive and must be kept cool and out of the sun.

Fresh water will kill them, so don't let them get wet.

They are an excellent bait for bottom feeders such as spot, croakers and sea mullet.

Cut them into ½ to one inch long pieces.

Bloodworms will live for several days if kept cool in a refrigerator or a cooler with ice.

SQUID

By them whole, fresh or frozen. Most tackle shops sell only frozen squid, but squid is one bait that freezes well.

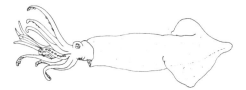

Anything will bite squid, but it is a top bait for flounders, croakers and trout.

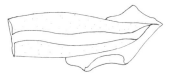

Squid must be cleaned. After thawing cut down the length of the body, scrape out viscera, and discard. Cut off tentacles. Small pieces may be used as bait for small fish, or the whole section of tentacles may be used as one bait for large flounders. Remove the skin by scraping with the edge of knife or by peeling.

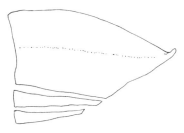

Cut the body into long, tapered wedges, and hook bait once through wide end.

SHRIMP

Buy them fresh or frozen. Fresh shrimp are usually available only during the warmer months. Avoid frozen shrimp that is freezer burned or colored a dark brown.

Shrimp can be cut into small pieces for bottom feeders, or used whole for puppy drum and trout.

Live shrimp is an excellent bait, but not very practical to use in the surf because of the difficulty in keeping them alive.

MOLE CRABS (SAND FLEAS)

Small crustaceans that burrow down into the sand as the waves recede. They are found between the low and high tide marks on the beach.

Not sold in bait and tackle shops, but they are plentiful during the summer months when they can be dug by hand.

Anything may bite them, and they are an excellent bait for pompano; especially soft shelled sand fleas.

Hook them once from the underside up through the shell.

They will stay alive for several days in a container of damp sand, kept in a cool place.

LIVE EELS

Live eels are most often used as bait in the surf north of the Chesapeake Bay. They are a favorite bait for striped bass and bluefish.

Eels can be kept alive in a small plastic bucket. Using an aerator will keep them alive longer.

Eels work best when hooked carefully through the head, on a fishfinder rig.

When on the beach, a handful of sand or a rag will help to grip a live eel.

CRABS

At different stages of their life blue crabs are called hard crabs, peelers, or soft crabs. Their new shells are soft, and harden after a short time if kept in salt water.

With soft crabs, the shell is completely soft. Simply cut the crab into bait-size pieces.

Peelers must have the hard, back shell removed.

Cut peelers and hard crabs in sections, and run the hook through the leg hole.

Crabs do not cast well. A strong, snap cast will tear off the crab. Use a smooth, lob cast when fishing with crabs.

LURES FOR CATCHING FISH IN THE SURF

TIPS:

- Lures are cast and retrieved with varying speeds and actions.

- "Match the Hatch"---use lures that imitate baitfish or food in the area. Size and color are important.

- Lures can be used with wire or monofilament leaders, but a heavy leader on a light lure will hinder the action.

SWIMMING PLUG

Good for striped bass, bluefish and weakfish. Used most frequently in the surf north of the Chesapeake Bay.

For stripers use at night, with a slow retrieve. Eel skins may be added to swimming plugs, for stripers.

A teaser (small hook dressed with bucktail), can be added on a short leader behind or ahead of a swimming plug.

Use dark colored plugs at night, lighter colors in daylight.

TOP WATER PLUG

Also called "Popping Plug". Retrieve quickly with a steady, rhythmic motion of the rod tip.

Use when fish are chasing bait and feeding on the surface.

HEAVY METAL SPOON

HOPKINS

STINGSILVER

Cast and retrieve at varying speeds.

Great lure for catching bluefish; use wire leaders.

Use a Stingsilver with no leader for Spanish mackerel.

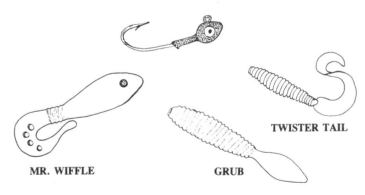

TWISTER TAIL

MR. WIFFLE   GRUB

LEAD HEAD JIG

Top lure for speckled trout, weakfish and puppy drum.

Add soft plastic tails, such as Mr. Wiffle, Twister Tails, or Grubs to change the color and action of the lure.

May be rigged in tandem.

Retrieve with an erratic, up-and-down jigging motion. Vary the retrieve, but usually slow is better.

Use mono leaders, or tie the lure directly to your line.

BUCKTAIL

Excellent lure for weakfish, speckled trout, stripers and flounder. They have lead heads, with hair or feathers tied over the hook.

Single or tandem bucktail rigs work well when "sweetened" with a piece of squid; shrimp or mullet.

Fish with a jigging action.

Don't use wire leaders.

MIRROLURE

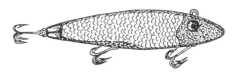

Good lure for speckled trout and puppy drum.

Cast the lure, let it settle for a couple seconds, and retrieve slowly.

Works best with light tackle.

KNOTS — WHICH TO USE, WHEN

TIPS:

- After tying a knot moisten it, and tighten it up slowly.

- Practice tying several types of knots before you get on the beach.

IMPROVED CLINCH KNOT

A good knot for making terminal connections, such as a snap swivel.

1. Pass line through the eye of the hook, swivel or lure. Double back and make five turns around the standing line.

2. Holding the coils in place, thread end of line around first loop above the eye, then through the big loop.

3. Hold tag end and standing line while pulling up coils. Make sure the coils are in a spiral, not lapping over each other. Slide tight against eye.

4. Clip tag end.

DROPPER LOOP

This forms a loop in the middle of an otherwise unknotted line, giving you a place to attach a hook, sinker or lure.

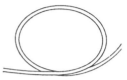

1. Form a loop in the line.

2. Pull one side of the loop down and begin turning it around the standing line. Keep points where turns are made open, so turns will gather equally on each side.

3. After eight to ten turns reach through center opening and pull remaining loop through. Keep your finger in this loop, so that the loop will not spring back.

4. Hold loop with teeth and pull both ends of line, gathering the turns on each side of loop.

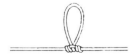

5. Set knot by pulling lines as tight as possible. Tightening the coils will make loop stand out perpendicular to line.

SPIDER HITCH

This is a fast, easy knot that creates a double-line leader.

1. Form a loop of the leader length desired. Near the point where the loop meets the standing line, twist a small section into a reverse loop.

2. Hold the small loop between thumb and forefinger, with thumb extended well above finger and the loop standing out beyond thumb.

3. Wind double line around both thumb and loop, taking five turns. Pass the remainder of large loop through the smaller one, and pull to make five turns. Unwind off thumb.

4. Pull turns around the base of the loop end tightly, and snip tag end.

SNELLING A HOOK

For making a common snell-hook-and-leader combination. Tie it to suite the length and strength needed for various types of bait fishing.

1. Insert one end of leader material through eye of hook and bring just past the turn and barb. Pass other end through eye in the opposite direction, leaving a large loop hanging down.

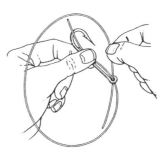

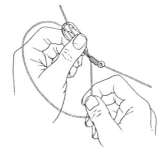

2. Holding both lines along the shank, wind tight coils around shank and both lines with the line hanging from the eye, moving from eye toward hook. Make 5 to 10 turns.

3. Move fingers to hold coil tightly in place. Pull leader extending from eye until entire loop has passed under coils.

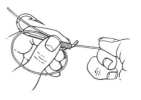

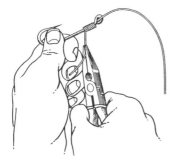

4. With the coils snugged neatly, use pliers to pull tag end, clinching the snell.

5. Clip off tag end and tie loop knot in end of leader.

RODS, REELS, ACCESSORIES

SPINNING RODS AND REELS

Spinning tackle is the most popular type of surf fishing gear because it is easy to learn how to use.

A spinning reel is mounted under the rod, and the rod is held in the angler's favored hand. A right-handed person will hold the rod in his right hand, and crank the reel with his left hand.

Spinning tackle is best suited for casting up to six ounces, and monofilament line of 20 pound test or lighter.

CONVENTIONAL RODS AND REELS

Conventional reels are mounted above the rod, and have a revolving spool. Effective use of conventional tackle requires some practice and careful "thumbing" of the line as it leaves the spool, to prevent backlashing.

Usually preferred by casters fishing with heavy weights and big chunks of bait for red drum and bluefish, and for casting heavy lures to striped bass and big bluefish.

ACCESSORIES AND OTHER GEAR

SAND SPIKE---a section of PVC pipe, pushed in the sand to hold a rod and reel. Laying a reel down in the sand may ruin it.

BUCKET---I use a five gallon bucket instead of a tackle box on the beach, to protect tackle from an unexpected wave, and blowing sand. Cut notches along the top for rigs and lures. Put other tackle in the bottom.

KNIFE---to cut bait and clean fish.

FISHING PLIERS---to remove hooks and cut line.

RAG---for wiping hands, need to drape over the top of the bucket to keep bait, fish and ice out of the sun.

CUTTING BOARD---for cutting bait. I made one out of ¼ inch plywood with rounded corners to fit in the bucket.

SURF BAG---used for carying lures, rigs and bait. It can easily be slung over a shoulder.

GAFF

I don't use a gaff in the surf, but it can be handy when landing large fish from a gradually sloping beach. Surf gaffs can be worn in a holster on your wader belt.

CAST NET---Excellent for catching fresh bait while fishing. Some states may require a license for using a cast net.

WADERS, FOUL WEATHER TOP---Wear chest waders when the water or air temperature prohibits fishing in shorts. Never wear waders without a belt or rope cinched above the waist to prevent water from rushing in over the top, in case of a fall in the surf. A foul weather top will keep you dry from rain and salt spray.

HAT, SUNSCREEN---I never go fishing during the day without applying a liberal amount of sunscreen SPF 15 or higher. The reflective properties of water and sand increase the likelihood of severe sunburn.

HOW TO LAND A FISH IN THE SURF

- When fighting a fish in the surf, keep the fish and your line directly in front of you.

- If the fish runs up or down the beach, move with it. If there are other fishermen on the beach, they will reel in their lines, or you can go over or under their line as you follow your fish.

- Don't walk backwards up the beach towards the dunes. Fight the fish at the edge of the surf.

- Most big fish that get away are lost only a few feet from shore. Breaking waves may pull the fish back into the ocean. Keep constant pressure on the fish, but be prepared to lower your rod tip suddenly, or walk to the fish if the sudden surge of a wave pulls on the fish.

- Don't pull hard on a fish against a receding wave, but maintain constant pressure, and let the next breaking wave "surf" the fish to you.

- Use surf gaffs carefully. Gaff a fish on a gradually sloping beach, where you are sure of your footing. Wading out too far on a steep beach can suddenly put you in water over your head.

TIDES, CURRENTS, AND WINDS

- Local tide charts are available (usually free) at tackle shops.

- On the Atlantic Coast there are two high tides and two low tides every day. A tidal "day" is actually 24 hours; 50 minutes long. During that tidal day high and low tides are spaced approximately six hours and a few minutes apart. The water level on the beach may change by several feet as the tide rises and falls through each cycle.

- For example, if high tide is at 5 a.m., the next low tide will occur around 11 a.m., and the following high tide will be a few minutes after 5 p.m. that same day. Fish may feed during a certain stage of the tide for several days in a row, if weather or water conditions do not change drastically.

- Around inlets, the volume of water flowing in and out of the inlet may cause a strong current. At some inlets the current may continue to flow in one direction after the tide stops running. This can be confusing to the novice surf-caster. Consult with your local tackle shop for information about currents and tides around inlets in the area.

- Wind velocity and direction can change water clarity, and how rough or calm the surf may be.

RELEASING FOR BETTER FUTURE FISHING

When you catch a fish that you are not going to keep as a trophy or for the table, release it. Fish are a limited resource, and carefully releasing them will help ensure the availability of future stocks.

RELEASE TECHNIQUES

Decide if you are going to keep the fish before you beach it.

Handle carefully, and release quickly. If possible wet your hands first to avoid removing the fish's protective slime coating.

If possible leave large fish in the water. Hold small fish firmly but gently, so as not to damage their internal organs. Never put your hands in the gills of a fish that is intended for release.

If the fish is hooked too deeply and the hook cannot be removed without injuring the fish, cut the leader as close to the hook as you can. The salt water will rust the hook out.

After removing the hook, hold the fish gently in the water until it swims away; avoid throwing the fish back into the ocean.

If a fish doesn't swim away immediately, gently move it forward (not backward and forward) in the water. This allows water to pass through it's gills.

Be careful of fish with teeth, fins, or barbs.

NOTES